The Battle of Verdun

A Captivating Guide to the Longest and Largest Battle of World War 1 That Took Place on the Western Front Between Germany and France

Free Bonus from Captivating History (Available for a Limited time)

Hi History Lovers!

Now you have a chance to join our exclusive history list so you can get your first history ebook for free as well as discounts and a potential to get more history books for free! Simply visit the link below to join.

Captivatinghistory.com/ebook

Also, make sure to follow us on Facebook, Twitter and Youtube by searching for Captivating History.

Contents

Introduction

Today, the landscape is marked by shell craters, pillboxes, and empty trenches. Mother Nature has tried to reclaim the terrain; the trees have grown again, and the ground is covered by lush green grass, but despite her best efforts, the scars on the landscape still remain, a constant reminder of the devastation and misery that was experienced here more than a century ago. And that is as it should be because the world should never forget what happened in this small corner of France. The battle scars on the landscape of Verdun are a testament to the horrors of a war that will live on in the collective memory of a nation forever, but they are also a memorial to the brave men who fought and died in the muddy fields defending their country and their countrymen from a foreign invader.

But Verdun was not just a battle; it was a seminal moment in French history. Every country that fought in the First World War experienced a defining battle or event that changed the course of their history or the way that they viewed themselves as a country. For the Ottoman Empire and the Anzacs (Australian and New Zealand Corps), it was Gallipoli;

for the British, the Battle of the Somme; for Russia, it came in the form of the October Revolution; and for France, it was Verdun. This is the battle that defines the First World War for France, but it cannot be viewed in isolation. It is part of a far greater story, influenced by the many events and battles that took place during this bloody time in Europe's history.

1916 was a watershed year in the First World War. It was then that the Allies realized that, without the aid of the United States, their prospects of winning, due to their resources and tactics, were limited. It was the last year that Russia would play any kind of significant role in the battle for dominance over Europe and be regarded as a powerful military force in the First World War. And finally, it was the year that Germany's hopes of outright victory finally vanished, and they had to accept that the Schlieffen Plan had failed.[1] Due to these factors, the war was virtually at a standstill. In their desperation to make progress and end the stalemate, the Germans would embark on a campaign against the French that would have devastating and far-reaching consequences for both sides.

Fought on the hills north of Verdun-sur-Meuse from February to December 1916, Verdun became the epicenter of what is now regarded as the costliest and deadliest offensive of the First World War and over time has come to symbolize the horror of war. No battle in the history of modern warfare has lasted as long and caused as much protracted suffering and misery as the Battle of Verdun. For 303 days, the hills, forests, and valleys of this picturesque corner of France rang and shook with the terrifying sound of artillery fire and was slowly turned into a hellish quagmire of blood, mud, and misery. "Mud, heat, thirst, filth, rats, the sweat smell of corpses" is how one eyewitness described it.

This once beautiful landscape of rolling hills and lush forests became hell on earth for the men who fought and died there. The soldiers were forced to live in trenches alongside the rotting bodies of their fallen comrades festering in stagnant water. They were constantly surrounded by the overpowering reek of death. An ever-present smell of death permeated everything: uniforms, hair, and even the very skin of the soldiers. It clung to their bodies, even when they left the front, and soon became known as the stench of Verdun. The soldiers digging trenches in the front lines even resorted to stuffing garlic cloves in their nostrils in an attempt to make the smell more bearable. If any place came close to being hell on earth, it had to be Verdun. One German soldier wrote to his parents that Verdun was an awful word, a place where "numerous people, still young and filled with hope, had to lay down their lives" and where their mortal remains decomposed in between trenches and in mass graves.[2]

Not only were the soldiers living in appalling conditions, but the constant shelling and relentless fire of the enemy were enough to drive battle-hardened men insane. A French captain described the front in one of his reports: "I have returned from the most terrible ordeal I have ever witnessed...the last two days in ice-cold mud – kept under relentless fire, without any protection whatsoever except for the narrow trench...I arrived with 175 men, I returned with 34 of whom several had half turned insane..."[3]

Verdun soon became more than just a strongpoint to be defended at all costs by the French, and the battle practically took on a demonic life of its own. The Germans lost sight of the strategic importance of the citadel, and for both sides, it became a matter of national pride and honor to be the victor at Verdun.

[1.] The Schlieffen Plan was drawn up in the early 20th century by Alfred Graf von Schlieffen, chief of the German Great General Staff from 1891 to 1905. The plan was developed to swiftly and effectively deal with a two-fronted war. The success of the Schlieffen Plan called for a swift military resolution on the Western Front so that Germany could then turn their full attention on Russia before the mighty Russian war machine had time to fully mobilize; this was predicated on the belief that it would take at least six weeks for the Russians to be in a position to attack Germany. This meant that, in the event of a two-fronted war, Germany would initially only need to place a nominal number of troops on the Eastern Front and could then use the bulk of their army and supplies to launch a swift attack through Belgium in the west. At the beginning of the 20th century, France had heavily fortified their border with Germany, and the Germans knew that a direct attack would take months. Therefore, Schlieffen advocated bypassing these fortifications and invading France via a fast march through neutral Belgium. Schlieffen was so confident in the strength of his plan that he calculated it would take a mere 42 days to complete, and when Germany was faced with a war on two fronts, they put the Schlieffen Plan into motion.

[2.] www.wereldoorlog1418.nl

[3.] www.wereldoorlog1418.nl

Chapter One - The Road to Verdun

By the end of 1915, the Allied Powers (Britain, France, Russia, Italy, and the United States) and the Central Powers (Germany, Austria-Hungary, the Ottoman Empire, and Bulgaria) had reached a virtual stalemate on the battlefields of Europe. The war had not gone the way that either side had predicted. The Western Front had become bogged down in the muddy trenches of Europe, a hallmark of the war, and the resulting deadlock stretched along a static front from the English Channel to Switzerland. The Germans had failed at the First Battle of Marne in August 1914 to deliver the hammer blow that would have ended the war on the Western Front, so both sides resorted to a war of attrition, trying to wear each other down and reduce the enemy's effectiveness through sustained and prolonged attacks. This was a war the likes of which the world had never experienced before, partly due to the scale of the conflict but also because of changes in military technology and weapons. At the turn of the 20th century, technology had dramatically changed the nature of warfare, but the military commanders of both the Allied and Central Powers had yet to grasp the true implications of these advances on the battlefield and on military strategy.

When the war broke out, both sides had expected it to be swift and brutal, and each had believed that their superior tactics and knowledge of warfare would ensure their ultimate victory. The Germans were confident that if they stuck to the Schlieffen Plan, they would quickly beat the French and still have time to prepare their attack on the Eastern Front before Russia could mobilize its mighty, but lumbering, war machine. Neither side had anticipated a long, protracted trench war, mostly due to the fact that this was a foreign concept at the time, and it is impossible to prepare for something that you cannot anticipate or have never even considered as a possibility.

Trenches[1], as part of a battle plan, were not new in 1914. The tactic of using entrenchments as cover from enemy fire and to seize positions from which to provide cover fire for the next phase of an attack had indeed been seen on the battlefields prior to the First World War. At the start of the war, the generals on both sides would have expected to use entrenchments to gain ground and drive the enemy back across their own battle lines. But these great military minds were a step out of tune with the reality of how much technology had changed modern warfare. They never anticipated that their armies would stay hunkered down in the trenches and that this would become the defining feature of the conflict.

The military leaders had assumed that artillery attacks would be able to destroy the trenches, or at least pin the troops down long enough to allow for an infantry or cavalry attack. This, however, was not the case, and on the Western Front, battles were won and lost in the trenches. But each victory came at a heavy cost, and the front line between Germany and France soon became a stalemate, with both sides suffering heavy casualties but gaining little advantage. As the Germans became bogged down in this bloody war of attrition and lost the advantage of being able to unleash the full might of their army on the Eastern Front, they were forced into the one situation that they had hoped to avoid—a long and drawn-out war on two fronts.

By the closing months of 1915, after almost 18 months of fighting, Germany had suffered 750,000 casualties in their attempt to neutralize

France. Germany's allies, the Austro-Hungarians, were not faring much better. From practically the start of the war, Austria-Hungary had become, to a large extent, a military satellite of Germany, who was the more dominant partner in the alliance. By 1916, the Austro-Hungarian Army was struggling with supply shortages, a high casualty rate, and low morale. They were almost totally reliant on German support and were becoming increasingly subordinate to the German generals and their ultimate war plan. The French, in their desperation to drive Germany backward and repulse the invaders from their soil, had sacrificed 300,000 men to their cause and a further 600,000 had been wounded, captured, or were missing. France's allies were not making much progress either: the mighty British navy had failed to wrest the Dardanelles from the Ottoman Empire, and the Gallipoli Campaign had ended in defeat for the Allies. The enormous Russian war machine had staggered from one defeat to the next without any major successes, and by 1916, it was slowly grinding to a halt as dissatisfaction grew amongst the Russian population and the empire itself teetered on the brink of revolution. The troops who had entered the war so willingly in 1914, thinking that it would all be over by Christmas, may have been disillusioned by what they experienced, but they were now also battle hardened and still possessed the will to continue to fight. Civilian resolution at the time also still matched military morale, and neither side was ready to admit defeat or negotiate a "stalemate" peace.

This was how things stood in Europe at the end of 1915, but everything was about to change as both sides were determined to break the deadlock and began carefully planning the next phase of their attack. These plans would culminate in two of the bloodiest and deadliest battles ever fought on French soil, and they would ultimately come to symbolize the unnecessary death and destruction of the First World War. By 1916, the stage was set for the Battle of Verdun and the Battle of the Somme, two battles that are inextricably intertwined in history.

On December 2, 1915, Joseph Joffre, the victor of the First Battle of the Marne, became supreme commander of the French Army. This made him the most powerful Allied commander in the war at the time.

Four days after being appointed to this position, Joffre held a historic meeting of the Allied commanders at his headquarters in Chantilly. It was at this meeting that the plans for a coordinated offensive by the Allies were set in motion. The offensive, planned for the summer of 1916, when for the first time the Allies would have an abundance of men, heavy artillery, guns, and ammunition, was to be a combined Franco-British "big push" designed to get the war moving again and hopefully drive the Germans back toward their own border.

The site that was chosen for this historic offensive was the area astride the river Somme. The attack was to be coordinated and led by the French. It would involve forty French and twenty-five British divisions. Joffre did not choose the most strategic point from which to launch the attack but rather a point in the Allied lines where the French and British armies met. And so, the Battle of the Somme was conceived. But at the same time, the Germans, under the command of General Erich von Falkenhayn, the chief of the German General Staff, were making their own plans. Unfortunately for the Allies, and more specifically the French, the Germans beat them to the punch and launched their attack first. The German target, however, was not the Somme but rather Verdun.

[1.] Trenches were intended to be simple temporary shelters designed to be packed with men fighting shoulder to shoulder. As the First World War progressed and the men started spending more time actually living in the trenches, the architecture of the trenches became more significant and elaborate. Before long, a maze of complex communications and supply trenches ran up to the front lines and connected to the battle trenches as both sides constructed an elaborate system of zigzagging frontline corridors, underground tunnels, traverses, firing recesses, and dugouts.

A well-designed trench was at least 2.5 meters (8 feet) deep so that men could walk upright and still be protected from enemy fire. The banked earth on the top of the trench facing the enemy was called the parapet and had a fire-step, where troops could stand to see out of the trenches and fire on the enemy. The rear lip of the trench was called the parados and protected the soldiers' backs from shells falling behind them. The floor of the trench was usually covered by wooden duckboards, and in later designs, the floor was raised on a wooden frame to provide for drainage. Trenches were further protected from assault by barbed wire, mines, netting, camouflaged pits, and other obstacles. Dugouts were constructed to be shell-proof and to resist both artillery bombardment and infantry assaults.

Chapter Two - The Citadel of Verdun

Verdun, called Virodunum in Roman times (dunum meaning fortress), is the largest city in the Meuse district of France. Situated at an important crossing point of the Meuse River, Verdun has played a crucial role in the defense of France throughout the centuries. It has always been coveted for its strategic position on the border of Belgium, Germany, and Luxembourg. Verdun's history as a fortified camp stretches all the way back to ancient times, and even Attila the Hun recognized its significance and believed that it was worth burning to the ground.

From the 14th to the 16th century, Verdun was a free imperial City in the Holy Roman Empire, which meant that the city was self-ruling and enjoyed a certain amount of autonomy. In the 17th century, Marshal Vauban built the city's famous citadel and made Verdun the most powerful fortress protecting France. It remained an important French garrison town until the 18th century. After the Franco-Prussian War of 1870, the French strengthened their chain of defenses along the border with Germany, and Verdun became the northernmost fortress of this chain. Germany annexed Alsace and part of Lorraine in 1871, and this placed Verdun a mere 45 km (28 miles) from the border with Germany. Ten defensive forts were immediately built around the city to protect the French border from a possible German invasion. Between 1880 and 1914, the French built a further 43 forts and strongholds centered around the citadel of Verdun, including Douaumont and Vaux. The fortifications around Verdun protected the left flank of the Meuse Barrier, and 4 km (2.5 miles) of underground galleries and tunnels were constructed between 1886 and 1893, and a further 7 km (4.3 miles) were added during the First World War. By the time the fortifications were complete, Verdun had a total of 19 major forts, armed with 75mm cannons and machine guns, and the landscape was dotted with pillboxes, concrete or steel circular shelters that housed heavy machine guns. It boasted a further 47 armored observation posts, and the garrison numbered 65,000 soldiers.

Unlike the open countryside around Flanders, a region in northern France and Belgium where several battles were fought during World War 1, and the Somme, Verdun was surrounded by steep hills and ridges which provided strong natural lines of defense. The key hills were fortified with three concentric rings of mighty underground forts and shellproof cellars that could house an infantry battalion. The infrastructure built below the citadel included accommodation for 2,000 soldiers, a communications station, a water supply network, and ammunition and powder magazines. Each fort was sited so that its guns could fire on enemy infantry if they captured the next fort in the line.

The forts were constructed with eight-foot-thick concrete that could withstand the German 420mm siege howitzers that were commonly nicknamed "Big Berthas." The most strategic forts, like Douaumont, were equipped with heavy artillery and machine gun turrets. Outlying blockhouses linked by subterranean tunnels meant that at Verdun the French could repel an attack from any direction. Verdun truly deserved its reputation as the most powerful fortress in Europe and arguably the world. In 1914, Verdun had provided a pivotal stronghold for the

French, and without it, Joffre may not have been able to hold back the Germans at Marne and save Paris. By the time fighting broke out in 1914, Verdun cast an imposing shadow over the surrounding landscape and posed a significant threat to any would-be invaders.

The Battle of Verdun was the longest single battle in the First World War, but it was not the first time that this city saw battle in the war. In September 1914, the Germans made an attempt to encircle Verdun and cut it off from France, and they almost succeeded. While the French were able to repel that attack, Verdun's defensive integrity was compromised. The two main railway lines into Verdun were destroyed by the Germans, leaving the city with just two supply routes, a single road and one narrow-gauge railway track from Bar-le-Duc in the west. The outlying Fort of Troydon was destroyed, and the fort at Camp des Romains was captured. The Germans also managed to capture the strategically useful ridge at Les Éparges, 24 km (15 miles) to the southeast of Verdun. But the German occupation of this high point was short-lived, and on February 17, 1915, a French counterattack reclaimed the Les Éparges ridge. By March 1915, infantry combat in the region had largely ground to a halt, and Verdun became one of the quieter sectors on the Western Front. This led to a growing complacency amongst the French troops garrisoned in the area and also meant that many of the fortress' guns were removed to be used elsewhere.

Chapter Three – The Significance of Verdun

By the time the Allies and the Germans clashed at Verdun, the war had been slowly grinding away for almost two years with no end in sight, and both sides were desperate for a breakthrough. The Allied and German generals were all looking for suitable sites to attack that would change the course of the war. There were many sites along the French frontline that the Germans could have randomly targeted which were clearly far easier targets to attack, so why did German Chief of General Staff Erick von Falkenhayn choose the heavily fortified citadel? To answer this question, one has to look at the significance of the site rather the actual geographic location.

Von Falkenhayn believed that the war would be won or lost in France, and he was also of the opinion that a war of attrition was Germany's best hope of victory. In December 1915, von Falkenhayn sent a lengthy message to Kaiser Wilhelm II, German emperor and king of Prussia, and nominal head of the German Armed Forces, in which he laid out his plan and argued that the only way to achieve total victory over the

Allies was to cripple the French Army. He expressed his opinion that while Britain was the most formidable of the Allied Powers, it could not be attacked directly, and their position at the Somme did not lend itself to a full-scale frontal offensive.

In von Falkenhayn's opinion, the only way to defeat the British was to defeat their allies. According to Falkenhayn, Russia and the Eastern Front no longer posed the greatest threat, and it was clear that the Italian Front was not going to play a major role in the outcome of the war, so that left France as the most significant target. He believed that Germany's best chance of a decisive victory would come in early 1916, and he intended to use the might of the German army to crush the French 96th Division before they were reinforced by the full deployment of British forces. Von Falkenhayn realized that if he could neutralize the French it would be almost impossible for the British to continue fighting on the Western Front without the support of their main ally. When von Falkenhayn conceived his battle plan, he chose Verdun with care and consideration because he intended to not only defeat the French but crush them both physically and mentally. He chose Verdun to make a statement.

Falkenhayn believed that the key to defeating France lay not in breaking through their lines but rather by attacking a target that the French would feel compelled to defend to the bitter end, a location where strategic necessity and national pride came together. The fabled citadel on the Meuse River offered von Falkenhayn exactly what he was looking for, a historically significant location in the French defenses. In order for his plan to succeed, von Falkenhayn needed to lure the French Army into the defense of an indefensible position that for physical and psychological reasons they would defend to the last, and Verdun, perched precariously at the tip of a long salient, was the perfect place.

Losing Verdun would not just have put the French at a strategic disadvantage; it would also have been a huge psychological and morale blow. Based on his knowledge of the history of France, Falkenhayn believed that if he threatened Verdun with a relatively modest force of nine divisions, he would draw the main weight of the French Army to the area, and he would then be able to use his heavy artillery to grind them to pieces from three sides. Von Falkenhayn's battle plan was relatively simple and called for the Germans to take the high ground and then use more than 1,200 artillery pieces in a continuous series of limited advances to draw the French reserves into the mincing machine of the German artillery and slowly obliterate them, while minimizing the exposure of the German infantry to battle and limiting German casualties. Von Falkenhayn's ultimate goal was to bleed France white in their attempt to defend the symbol of Verdun. Crown Prince Wilhelm II, eldest child of Kaiser Wilhelm and Empress Augusta, and the last crown prince of the German Empire, was chosen to lead the German army at the Battle of Verdun.

When von Falkenhayn selected Verdun as his primary target, he most likely knew that the city was not as heavily fortified as it once was. His intelligence would have informed him that by February 1916 the fortress' defenses were, despite its reputation, no longer what they had been at the outbreak of the war. Joffre had evacuated the infantry garrisons from the forts surrounding Verdun and removed many of the guns. The troops that had remained, thinking that Verdun was impregnable and not a likely target for an attack after they had repelled the Germans in early 1915, had been lulled into a false sense of security. The trenches surrounding Verdun were not that well-constructed and were only manned by 34 battalions. The Crown Prince, on the other hand, had 72 battalions of elite troops waiting to attack Verdun. He also had over 800 guns, including 26 long-range guns.

But even the best-laid plans have their shortcomings, and one cannot plan for every eventuality. While the Germans were preparing for their attack on Verdun in January 1916, the French were so focused on their plans for an offensive at the Somme that they almost did not see what was happening. Fortunately, a French intelligence officer discovered the buildup of German troops on the right bank of the Meuse on February 11, 1916. This discovery forced the French to divert some of their troops away from planning their offensive at the Somme and toward a defensive position at Verdun.

Over the next ten days, French officers organized a motorized supply chain on an unprecedented scale and used more than 3,000 trucks to move materials, supplies, thousands of troops, and dozens of guns to Verdun to defend against the now anticipated German attack. Fortunately for the French, Mother Nature also appeared to be on their side, and the German attack was delayed by nine days due to bad weather conditions. This delay allowed the French to strengthen their hastily prepared positions, and the defenses at Verdun were shored up in the nick of time.

The shelling of Verdun started at dawn on February 21, 1916, marking the beginning of a battle that lasted 303 days and turned the surrounding countryside into hell on earth.

Chapter Four – The First Phase of the Battle of Verdun

When you hear the whistling in the distance your entire body preventively crunches together to prepare for the enormous explosions...Even nerves of the hardest steel, are not capable of dealing with this kind of pressure. The moment comes when the blood rushes to your head, the fever burns inside your body and the nerves, numbed with tiredness, are not capable of reacting to anything anymore. – Paul Dubrulle, a thirty-four-year-old French soldier's description of the horrors of the bombardment of Verdun.[1.]

The Battle of Verdun (codenamed Gericht, or Judgement by the Germans) commenced at dawn on February 21, 1916, as 380mm German naval guns opened fire with an intense and unprecedented ten-hour artillery bombardment. Even on the shell-saturated Western Front, a shelling of this magnitude had never been experienced before. The targets of the shells falling deep behind French lines were bridges over the Meuse, the Bishop's Palace at Verdun, and the city's railway station. Hundreds of German artillery pieces and mortars also unleashed their terrifying firepower on the trenches. The impact of the shells on the French lines was devastating, and in places, the hastily and relatively poorly constructed French trenches were obliterated under the barrage of firepower, and countless soldiers were buried alive as the earthen walls collapsed inward. Soldier's bodies were ripped apart by shrapnel or torn to pieces by explosives, and their unrecognizable remains scattered across the landscape.

The continual thunder of the barrage could be heard 240 km (149 miles) away, and the once familiar landscape of forests and hills surrounding the picturesque city of Verdun was recontoured by the force of the explosions ripping up the earth. Even for the most battle-hardened French soldiers, the experience was overwhelming, and survival became the only goal of the day as they hunkered down in trenches, shell holes, and dug-outs, hoping to survive the next onslaught and waiting for darkness to fall and the nightmarish day to end. During the terrifying bombardment, the 56th and 59th Divisions of the French Army lost approximately 60% of their men.

At 4:45 p.m., after a relentless bombardment that lasted for more than nine hours, the German artillery guns fell silent, and the first soldiers of the German 5th Army, under the command of the Crown Prince, left the safety of their trenches and advanced toward the French frontlines. This probing attack by small groups of German troops, armed with grenades and flamethrowers and supported by the cover fire of machine guns, was meant to test the strength of the remaining French defenses, and some positions succumbed without a fight. But much to the surprise of the Germans, when the shelling eventually stopped, the dazed French survivors in many of the trenches did not just retreat to safety but rather did their best to hold the line. These small pockets of resistance were the first indications of the lengths to which the French were prepared to go to to hold Verdun.

On the afternoon of February 21, as the straggling French troops faced the highly organized German 21st Division of the 42nd Brigade, they did so with such astonishing bravery and tenacity that the Germans did not advance as swiftly as they had anticipated. They were forced to fight for every inch of ground as small groups of French soldiers fought bravely until they were killed, seriously wounded, or ran out of ammunition. One of the French units to bear the brunt of this brutal artillery attack on the first day of the Battle of Verdun was Driant's chasseurs (light infantry).

At the outbreak of the First World War, Emile Driant, a retired French Army officer, was recalled to the army as a captain. He was quickly promoted to the rank of lieutenant colonel and given command of 1,200 men of the 56th and 59th Chasseur Reserve Battalion. In 1915, being aware that Verdun may be targeted by the Germans, Driant criticized Joffre for removing artillery guns and troops from the defensive line around France's famous citadel. Despite Driant's dire warnings, no guns or troops were returned to these crucial positions. In the end, Driant was proven correct, but this would have been cold comfort for him and his men when they were caught up in the devastation of the first day of shelling at Verdun.

During this terrifying assault, Driant and his men fought valiantly to hold a large section of the Bois des Caures (Des Caures Wood) for as long as possible to buy the French high command much-needed time to rush more troops to the threatened sector and for the men in the forts to prepare a more effective defense. But their gallant effort came at a huge price. The chasseurs held the line for almost two days before they were outflanked and outgunned, and their position finally became untenable. Driant ordered the survivors to conduct a fighting withdrawal. As the men withdrew, picking their way across the scarred landscape of shattered tree stumps and deep shell holes, Driant stopped to give a field dressing to a wounded soldier and was shot through the head and killed. Of his 1,200 men, only a handful of officers and approximately 500 fighting men, many of them seriously wounded, managed to make it back to the safety of the French lines. Several other battalions and regiments along the French line fought equally as hard as Driant's chasseurs and ensured that the Germans made little progress on the first day.

The devastated landscape with its collapsed trenches, deep shell holes, and mighty trees torn asunder and scattered across the ground also aided the French defensive lines, as it created a complicated and difficult terrain for the German attackers to move across. Although the Germans were surprised by the French defense on the first day of the battle, as they could not conceive that anything or anyone could have survived the bombardment, let alone still have the energy and wherewithal to fight, they were confident that their superior numbers and firepower would still enable them to take Verdun within a couple of days. By the end of the first day, despite their fierce resistance, the Germans had penetrated the French defensive line in several places and occupied the Bois d'Haumont (Haumont Wood).

The next day, the bombardment began again, and while it seemed impossible that anyone could survive a second day of continuous and methodical artillery assaults, they did. With a heroic tenacity that would come to embody the French defense of Verdun, the surviving soldiers hunkered deep in their trenches until the shelling ended and then continued to defend their positions as best they could from what remained of the trenches. On the afternoon of February 22, the Germans' first main infantry wave attacked, and the French front line buckled under the relentless pressure as the village of Haumont was razed by artillery fire. But once again, the unanticipated French resistance and tenacity prevented the Germans from pressing their advantage, and they were forced to pull back.

The morning of February 23 again began with a bombardment of the French lines by German artillery. By now, there was mounting chaos and confusion in the French defensive lines. Telephone lines were knocked out by the shelling, and messengers running between commanders were not getting through to their destinations. Entire units had been scattered along the line, and one by one, the French batteries began to fall silent. As the French were forced back, they bent under the intense German assault, but their lines did not break wide open, and they finally managed to use their artillery to halt part of the German advance at Samogneux. Despite the valiant effort of the French soldiers in the trenches, by nightfall on February 23, the villages of Brabant-sur-Meuse, Wavrille, and Samogneux had all fallen to the Germans.

In three days, the Germans had overrun the first line of the French defenses, and thousands of French troops, placed in untenable positions, were lost. It certainly began to look like von Falkenhayn's plan was working and that the Germans would achieve an outright victory at Verdun. February 24, 1916, was a particularly bleak day in French history as the Germans gained even more ground at Verdun. A fresh division of French defenders, ill-prepared for the battle they faced, quickly broke under the relentless German bombardment, and the entire second line of French defenses fell within a matter of hours. On that fateful day, the Germans gained more ground than they had in the previous three days put together. It looked like the German army was on the advance for the first time since the Battle of Marne. After further intense fighting, the Germans took Beaumont, the Bois des Fosses, and the Bois des Caurieres.

However, between the Germans and the town of Verdun, there still lay the line of forts, including Douaumont, the largest and highest of the nineteen forts protecting the city of Verdun. At this point in the battle, everything appeared to be going the way of the Germans. The French found themselves under intense pressure, but still, they held firm and fought tooth and nail to defend their famous citadel, making the Germans work for every meter of ground they gained. The French clung to the hope that the German advance would be halted by the forts and that Douaumont would stand strong. But the Germans pressed forward relentlessly, and on February 25, they pulled off one of the greatest successes of the First World War. Only five days into the Battle of Verdun, the German forces captured the mighty Fort Douaumont, the jewel in the crown of Verdun. This feat was achieved by several small pockets of the 24th Brandenburg Regiment, under the command of Lieutenant Eugen Radtke, who captured the fort without losing a single man or firing a single shot.

The Germans advanced steadily, and with the support of machine gun fire from the edge of Bois Hermitage, they rushed the French position at Côte 347 (Hill 347). The French were quickly outflanked and forced to retreat to the village of Douaumont. The Germans pursued them until they came under machine gun fire from the roof of Douaumont church. At the same time, the German artillery was also bombarding the area. To avoid the strafing machine gun fire of the French and the shelling from their own troops, two small groups of German soldiers took cover in the woods and in a ravine that led toward Fort Douaumont. Both parties made their way toward the fort, which they assumed would be heavily fortified and well-guarded. They did not realize that the French garrison at Fort Douaumont was only made up of a small maintenance crew of approximately 25 men, under the command of a French warrant officer by the name of Chenot.

As they advanced, the German troops used flares to signal to their artillery to stop the bombardment of the area, but because of poor visibility due to snow and the advancing twilight, the flares were not seen by the German artillery. However, the French machine guns in the village of Douaumont fell silent as the French troops mistook the German flares for those of French Zouaves (light infantry regiments) retreating from Côte 378. The German soldiers cut through the wire around the fort and were able to reach the northeastern end of the building. They found their way inside and moved quietly down the central Rue de Rempart until they found the small French garrison on a lower level and took them prisoner without a shot being fired. In France, the surrender of Fort Douaumont was regarded as a national disaster. In Germany, church bells rang throughout the country to celebrate the capture of Douaumont.

Just as the situation was looking most dire for the French, on February 27, Mother Nature once again played her hand in favor of the Allies. The thawing snow around Verdun turned the ground into a swamp, making some German artillery batteries unserviceable and stranding others in the mud. After their relentless push forward for almost a week to gain as much territory as possible, the German infantry was beginning to suffer from exhaustion, and the unexpectedly high casualty rate was taking a toll on morale. The German infantry's swift advance also meant that many of the troops had moved beyond the range of their artillery's covering fire, and the muddy conditions made it almost impossible to move the heavy guns forward to keep pace with the infantry. On February 29, the German advance was halted at Douaumont by the French 33rd Infantry Regiment and fortuitously heavy snowfall.

After the fall of Douaumont, the French high command finally realized the seriousness of the situation at Verdun, and Joffre sent General Philippe Pétain, a master of the art of defense, to command the French troops. His orders were to hold Verdun, whatever the cost. As the German army prepared for the next phase of their attack, General Philippe Pétain, having been given the formidable task of holding the right bank of the Meuse, was busy shoring up the French defenses. The French commander knew that if the east bank of the Meuse was lost, then all would be lost. If Pétain could not hold this strategic position, then the French would not be able to hold Verdun. And if Verdun fell, the effect on morale would be catastrophic, and the French leadership doubted the nation would survive the blow.

General Pétain's reputation as a master of defense was well-deserved, and he wasted no time preparing for a long and arduous battle to hold the citadel. Pétain brought a fresh army, the French 2nd Army, to fight at Verdun and stabilize the front. 90,000 men and 23,000 tons of ammunition were bought to the frontline from the railhead at Bar-le-Duc. Pétain valued the lives of his men, and he did not push his troops into the vulnerable front lines where they would be easy targets for the Germans. He rather organized them to defend a series of mutually supported strongpoints and consolidate the existing lines. He ordered that no attempts be made to retake Fort Douaumont, but the forts that remained in French hands were rearmed and stocked with enough supplies to withstand a German siege. Pétain rotated his units through the front lines with regularity, ensuring that his troops did not spend long periods of time at the sharp end of the front. Pétain also greatly increased the number of artillery pieces at Verdun and began to subject the Germans to the same levels of bombardment that the French had been suffering under.

One of the keys to French survival at Verdun was the "Voie Sacrée," or Sacred Way. This was the single road into Verdun that enabled the French to keep their troops supplied with ammunition and other vital supplies. The Voie Sacrée, simply called La Route at the time, was a 65 km long, 7 meter-wide (40 miles long, 23 feet wide) road connecting Verdun and Bar-le-Duc, the nearest primary connection to the French rail network. By 1916, this road was in a pretty bad state and under constant threat of bombardment by the Germans. Pétain set about repairing the road and keeping this lifeline operating day and night.

The route was divided into zones and numerous Territorial Divisions, each headed by an army officer who was tasked with keeping the road repaired and the traffic moving. Stone quarries were opened nearby, and the Territorial soldiers were responsible for breaking the stone and shoveling it into holes and under trucks as they passed. 700,000 tons of stone and debris were thrown onto the road during the Battle of Verdun to maintain its surface during the long months of the campaign.

At the outbreak of the war in 1914, motorized technology was not expected to play a major role in the war, so the French Army had less than 200 trucks. Like most armies of the time, they were more reliant on horses and railways for transport. To keep the supplies flowing to Verdun along the Sacred Way, the French Army requisitioned every truck it could find. Much like the famous Marne Taxis that brought much-needed French reinforcements from Paris to the First Battle of Marne in September 1914, it was once again motorized transport that helped rescue the French. The Voie Sacrée was reserved for motor transport, so infantry troops and horse-drawn artillery had to make use of the fields alongside the road. Seven Nieuport aerial fighter squadrons were used to defend the road from aerial bombardment, and several airstrips were established in the area exclusively for this purpose.

Supplying Verdun along the Voie Sacrée was a mammoth undertaking. The flow of trucks along the route never ceased. Day and night, they trundled up and down the road, bringing vital supplies and fresh troops to the front. The trucks, traveling at an average speed of 25 km (15.5

miles) per hour, passed along the road at a rate of one every 14 seconds. Trucks were not permitted to stop or pass vehicles in front of them, and any vehicle that broke down was simply pushed off the road so as not to halt the endless flow of traffic. Unlike the Germans, who kept the same divisions in place throughout the ten-month Battle of Verdun, Pétain rotated his troops to keep them fresh. Every day, 15–20,000 men and 2,000 tons of munitions made their way along the Voie Sacrée. By December 1916, almost two and a half million men had traveled this famous road. Despite the constant threat of heavy shelling, the French were able to keep the Voie Sacrée open and the front supplied with indispensable provisions, troops, and munitions. The Sacred Way delivered the essential lifeblood the French so dearly needed to defend Verdun, and in the first week of March alone, 190,000 soldiers marched into hell along this route.

[1.] Taylor, AJP, A History of World War One, p 121

Chapter Five – The Battle of Verdun Gets Bogged Down in the Trenches

Once General Pétain arrived at Verdun, things began to unravel for the Germans; however, it was not due to Pétain's brilliant leadership but rather because of their own doing. The Germans made the fatal mistake of changing tactics in the middle of the campaign. Had they stuck to von Falkenhayn's original plan, the Battle of Verdun may have had a very different outcome, but that was not to be.

From the start, von Falkenhayn's battle plan had been to restrict his offensive to the right bank of the Meuse in a concentrated attack on the French forts. His entire strategy was based on a war of attrition, drawing the French into an untenable position and then bleeding them white through continuous heavy artillery fire while minimizing German losses. The Crown Prince, however, had other ideas, and he wanted to attack both banks of the Meuse River simultaneously. At the end of February, buoyed by their initial success, the Crown Prince was even more eager to commit the German 5th Army to a greater offensive action.

As with every offensive on the Western Front, the German attack was inevitably getting bogged down in the muddy fields, and they were losing far more men than von Falkenhayn had ever anticipated. Thousands were sacrificed daily to gain little more than a few hundred feet. As the Germans began taking heavy fire from French guns along the Meuse, von Falkenhayn reluctantly agreed to extend the offensive across to the left bank of the river to clear this threat and once again reduce German casualties. To this end, he agreed to release more of his corps at the beginning of March, marking a deadly escalation in the Battle of Verdun. The seizure of ground, rather than strategic targets, now became the priority for the Germans, and by early March, casualties on both sides were rising, but little headway was being made.

On March 6, the Germans once again renewed their offensive and attacked the left bank of the Meuse, pushing toward a small ridge known as Mort-Homme (Dead Man's Hill), which sheltered batteries of French field guns that hindered the German troops' progress toward Verdun on the right bank of the Meuse. Using a two-pronged attack, planned by General Heinrich von Gossler, the 6th Reserve Corps and the 10th Reserve Corps, supported by 25 heavy artillery batteries, were tasked with capturing a line from south of Avocourt through Côte 304 to Mort Homme and Côte 265. This area was a key target for the Germans because it would put them in a position to destroy the French artillery on the west bank of the Meuse.

The first phase of the attack on Mort-Homme and Côte 265 was planned for March 6, and the assault on Avocourt and Côte 304 was to take place on March 9. The fight to gain ground was fierce, and the area around the Mort-Homme soon became the center of bitter backward and forward fighting. After storming the Bois des Corbeaux and taking it on March 7, the Germans quickly lost it to the French again the very next day. The Germans then launched another attack on March 9, capturing Bois des Corbeaux for the second time. The two-pronged German assault on the west bank was supported by 25 heavy artillery batteries, and the German bombardment of Côte 304 was so intense that it reduced the height of the hill from 304 m (997 feet) to 300 m (984 feet). But the Germans on the east bank of the Meuse were still taking heavy fire from the French guns that were operational behind Côte de Marre and Bois Burrous. The German artillery on Côte 265 was also being subjected to systematic artillery fire by the French, and the Germans had to change their attacks from large operations to narrow-fronted assaults in order to gain limited objectives. Even once the Germans finally managed to take the ridge at Mort-Homme, they were still stymied by the French artillery guns on Côte 304. This meant that more fresh German divisions were thrown into the fray to take this next ridge. By March 14, the Germans had finally taken parts of the ridge at Mort-Homme, Côte 304, and Cumieres. An objective that the Germans had hoped to achieve in a day had taken them a full week. This one small sector of the battlefield typified what the campaign to take Verdun had turned into—an endless round of attack, defend, and counterattack. Fighting tooth and nail to take a strategic point only to lose it again within a few days. This certainly was the war of attrition that von Falkenhayn had planned, but he had not expected the Germans to pay as high a price as the French.

By March, the German attacks no longer had the element of surprise, and they now faced a well-supplied and determined French Army that was willing to defend Verdun to the bitter end. The German artillery was still managing to inflict devastating attacks on the French defensive line, but it came at a heavy cost as the French artillery returned fire, killing many Germans and cutting battalions off from their supply lines. Continuous artillery fire allowed the German infantry to make small advances, but the French used the same tactics to launch counterattacks.

Soon, Verdun was following the typical course of all First World War battles, and both sides were once again bogged down in the trenches. Adding to the misery, conditions worsened as persistent rain fell throughout March and April, turning the battlefield into a quagmire. Soldiers were sleeping and eating next to rotting corpses, and the battlefield had become a reeking mass of decomposing bodies.

"Everyone who searches for cover in a shell hole, stumbles across slippery, decomposing bodies and has to proceed with smelly hands and smelly clothes" was how one soldier described the hell that Verdun had turned into. And so, the battle raged on for month after month with neither side being able to turn their successes into outright victory. Villages were taken one day by the Germans only to be lost again days later. The battle had turned into a bloody stalemate of attack and counterattack.

As conditions continued to worsen, in many places there were no longer even trenches to defend; in their places were merely clusters of shell holes where isolated groups of men lived and died defending their positions. Despite the heroic sacrifices of the French Army, day by day, the Germans moved ever closer to the town of Verdun. By the end of March 1916, the French had lost almost 89,000 men, and the Germans weren't faring much better. Despite von Falkenhayn's best efforts to limit German casualties, they too had lost over 80,000 fighting men. This was not at all what von Falkenhayn had intended when he laid out his battle plan only a few months earlier.

In late April, General Robert Nivelle took over control of the French forces from Pétain and began a large-scale counteroffensive. This allowed the Germans to return to von Falkenhayn's original plan and launch their final push toward Verdun, but it was too late for the strategy to be implemented successfully. The Germans had long since lost sight of the strategic importance of Verdun, and the battle had practically taken on a demonic life of its own. Honor had become so significant to both sides that it was impossible for either side to disengage without suffering a devastating and humiliating defeat. The Germans knew if they did not push forward, they would be forced to withdraw to where they had started in February 1916, and they were not prepared to do this.

At the end of May 1916, with no foreseeable end in sight at Verdun, Joseph Joffre met with Sir Douglas Haig, commander of the British forces who had been tasked with planning the Battle of Somme after the French had been forced to turn their attention to defending Verdun.

Joffre urged Haig to advance the date of the Somme offensive. At first, Haig was resistant to this idea. He had planned to launch the offensive in mid-August and was determined to stick to his timeline. But Joffre argued that there would be no French Army left by then, and so eventually, Haig reluctantly agreed to move up his attack to the start of July. The basic strategic purpose of the Somme offensive was now to relieve the pressure on the French at Verdun and kill as many Germans as possible in the process.

Chapter Six – A Summer in Hell

June bought with it not just the summer heat and relentless flies but also the deadliest and most intense phase of fighting as the Germans threw their entire weight behind an attack concentrated along a front that was little more than three miles wide. In early June, the Germans attacked the Fort of Vaux, the second most important of the great forts, which was situated at the northeastern extremity of the French line. Vaux had been bombarded by approximately 8,000 shells per day since the beginning of the Verdun offensive, and after a final German assault on June 1, 10,000 German soldiers were able to occupy the top of the fort. Fighting, however, continued underground as 600 French soldiers, under the command of Major Sylvain Eugene Raynal, heroically and defiantly held up the main force of the German 5th Army for a whole week before they ran out of water and were forced to surrender. The taking of Vaux was a significant victory for the Germans, but it also proved to be their last successful attack at Verdun.

Due to the policy of troop rotation introduced under the command of General Pétain, by June 15, 66 divisions (approximately 75%) of the

French Army had seen action at Verdun. The Germans had only used 43 divisions. The French guns had fired over ten million field artillery rounds, and yet despite this enormous expenditure of resources and horrific loss of life, little had changed on the front, and neither side had made any significant gains. On the left bank, the Germans advanced from Côte 304, Mort-Homme, and Cumieres to threaten Avocourt and Chattancourt. But heavy rains slowed their progress toward Fort Souville, which dominated a hill 1 km (0.62 miles) southeast of the town of Fleury. For the next two months, both sides attacked and counterattacked in the area without any significant gains. As the two opposing armies continued to scrabble for an advantage at Verdun, preparations for the offensive at the Somme added to the pressure on both sides to push for a hasty and conclusive resolution.

Just as Vaux fell, the Allied summer offenses were unleashed, with the Russians launching the Brusilov Offensive and the British attacking at the Somme. Finally, the tide began to turn in favor of the French as the Germans were forced to redirect troops to deal with these new threats. In the east, Russian General Brusilov led an attack against the Austro-Hungarian Army with forty Russian divisions. Initially, this campaign was a success, and even though it later faltered, it did achieve one vital goal, and that was to draw German forces away from Verdun. Falkenhayn was forced to transfer badly needed troops from the battlefield of Verdun to support Germany's failing ally.

This, however, did not end the German assault on Verdun; it was merely a reprieve for the French. On June 22, the Germans fired 116,000 phosgene gas shells at the French lines as they advanced toward Fort Souville, a position that had been bombarded by over 38,000 shells and was the last ridge before Verdun. Capturing this position, one of the main German objectives since the start of the offensive, would have given the Germans control of the high ground overlooking Verdun. The gas fired at the French lines caused 1,600 casualties. With soldiers struggling to breathe, vomiting, and suffering from blurred vision, much of the French artillery fell silent. This enabled the Germans to capture the Ouvrage de Thiaumont and the

Ouvrage de Froidterre, and overrun the villages of Fleury (Fleury changed hands sixteen times from June 23 to August 17) and Chapelle Sainte-Fine. Chapelle Sainte-Fine marked the farthest point the Germans reached during the Battle of Verdun. When the Germans took the town of Fleury, General Nivelle issued the now famous Order of the Day that ended with the words, "They shall not pass!" (Ils ne passeront pas!)

The Germans were now within 5 km (3 miles) of the citadel of Verdun, close enough to the city that they were able to fire machine gun rounds into the streets. Yet still the French fought on, but morale was now dangerously low, and no one knew just how much more they could take. Four French divisions were diverted from the Somme to Verdun, and the French were able to finally halt the German advance, pushing them back and retaking Chapelle Sainte-Fine. Finally, on June 24, the rumble of British heavy guns could be heard in Verdun. The seven-day preliminary bombardment of the Somme had at long last begun. On June 25, with both sides suffering from heavy fatigue, Knobelsdorf, the Chief of Staff of the German 5th Army, suspended their attack at Verdun.

Once fighting broke out at the Somme, the pressure lifted slightly on Verdun, although the bloody fighting would continue for almost another six months. On July 11, the Germans mounted one last desperate effort to capture Verdun. They once again focused their attention on Fort Souville. The attack began with a preliminary bombardment on July 9 with 60,000 gas shells being fired at this strategic position, but this had little effect because the French had been outfitted with M2 gas masks that were more effective at protecting them from the effects of gas than previous models had been. The attack by three German divisions began two days later, but the infantry became bottlenecked on the road leading to Fort Souville and was an easy target for the French artillery. The German soldiers who managed to survive the bombardment were shot at by sixty French machine gunners stationed at Fort Souville. On July 12, a handful of German troops did manage to reach a ridge from where they could stare down upon the city of Verdun. They could see the rooftops of houses and buildings and even the spire of the imposing Verdun Cathedral, but this was as close as they would ever get to Verdun. On the evening of July 11, Crown Prince Wilhelm received orders from von Falkenhayn to cease attacking Verdun and go on the defensive. The French 2nd Army finally gained artillery superiority in the area, and Nivelle was able to launch a counterattack and begin to slowly retake lost ground, as the fighting continued to rage backward and forward between the French and German lines.

By the end of August, von Falkenhayn was replaced as Chief of the General Staff by the dynamic duo of Paul von Hindenburg and Erich Ludendorff. In September, General Charles Mangin, a gifted strategist who held the French defensive line from Fleury to the right bank of the Meuse, proposed a plan to Nivelle that he hoped would finally liberate Verdun. On October 21, the French initiated their First Offensive Battle of Verdun with the aim of recapturing Fort Douaumont. The attack started with an artillery barrage across a broad front followed by an infantry assault with three divisions advancing behind a creeping artillery barrage—a tactic whereby artillery shells were fired just in front of advancing lines to aid their progress. By the evening of October 24, the French had retaken Douaumont, and by November 2, they retook the fort at Vaux as well.

In order to exploit their success, the French planned an attack for December 5 with the intention of retaking the entire former second French line that had been lost very early on in the battle. Preparations for the attack began on November 29 with a 750 gun barrage. Bad weather, however, put an end to this assault, delaying the French attack and effectively ending their element of surprise. This gave the Germans the opportunity to launch an aggressive counterattack on December 6. Fortunately for the French, on December 9, the weather turned again and what followed was an artillery duel between the two armies.

At 10:00 a.m. on December 15, the final showdown of the Battle of Verdun began, but the Germans launched their counter barrage a few vital minutes too late, and four French divisions were able to attack their lines. By nightfall, the French had captured and destroyed 115 German guns, and more than 9,000 men had been taken prisoner. This engagement, later known as the Battle of Louvemont, ended on December 18 with the capture of Chambrettes. This marked the end of the Battle of Verdun.

Conclusion

By Christmas 1916, both the Battle of Verdun and the Battle of the Somme were over. But both campaigns had truly been hell on earth for the men who fought and died in those muddy fields. Verdun was conceived and executed by von Falkenhayn to be a bloody war of attrition, and he certainly achieved that goal but not in the way that he had envisioned. Von Falkenhayn was correct in his assessment that France would defend their famous citadel to the bitter end, but he underestimated their strength and resilience, and this ultimately led to the German defeat at Verdun.

For months, the French fought tooth and nail just to stay in the battle, but finally, through strategic troop management and the effective use of new tactics based on specialist infantry sections armed with light machine guns, rifle grenades, mortars, and light field guns, combined with efficient logistics and the resilience of the men in the trenches, the French secured victory at Verdun. Unfortunately, it came at a tremendous cost. The Germans suffered over 330,000 casualties, and the French lost approximately 370,000 to death and injury. Von Falkenhayn had planned to bleed France white with a battle of attrition, but he had never anticipated that Germany would bleed as heavily.

The landscape of the area has also been forever altered, and nine villages—Beaumont, Bezonvaux, Cumieres, Douaumont, Fleury, Haumont, Louvemont, Ornes, and Vaux—were entirely destroyed and never rebuilt. An area covering 170 square kilometers (65 square miles) on the Verdun ridge is still declared a red zone due to the presence of unexploded ordnance (unexploded bombs or explosive remnants of war). It is estimated that over ten million shells remained buried in the ground around Verdun after the battle ended, and forty tons of unexploded munitions are still being removed from the area annually.

The Battle of Verdun also had serious strategic consequences for the remainder of the war. The original Allied plan to defeat the Germans through a series of large-scale coordinated attacks, referred to as the "Big Push," led by the French lay in tatters. The Battle of Verdun had inflicted massive damage on the French Army, drastically reducing their number of fighting men, and this meant that ultimately Britain would have to lead the "Big Push" on the Western Front.

The Battle of Verdun was the longest, bloodiest, and costliest battle of the First World War, and by the time it over, it had decimated both the German and French armies, and the scars of the battle on the French national psyche can still be felt to this day. The French nation will never forget the sacrifices their brave sons made on the battlefield to hold Verdun and ultimately ensure their freedom.

Remembering the Fallen

The Battle of Verdun took the lives of approximately 300,000 predominately French and German soldiers, but tragically the bodies of 160,000 men have never been found. Blown apart or buried deep in the French soil, these men have no known resting place, but they are remembered and honored in the various memorials in and around Verdun.

Several monuments have been erected in the area to honor the fallen.

The Monument à la Victoire et aux Soldats de Verdun was designed by architect Léon Chesnay and stands in the very heart of the city. It is topped by a statue of Emperor Charlemagne dressed as a warrior and leaning on his sword.

The Monument aux Enfants de Verdun Morts pour la France represents five soldiers, an infantryman, an engineer, an artilleryman, a rider, and a soldier from the Territorial Army, standing shoulder to shoulder.

The Monument de la Voie Sacrée et de la Voie de la Liberté stands at the crossroads of the route linking Verdun to Bar-le-Duc and Argonne, marking the vital road that kept the French Army supplied.

The remains of the soldiers who died on the battlefields of Verdun are interned in 19 cemeteries in the area. The largest one is the Douaumont Ossuary and Necropolis, created by the bishop of Verdun, Monsignor Ginisty, who wanted to ensure that the men who sacrificed their lives at Verdun were given a decent resting place. The top of the Douaumont hill is dominated by the Douaumont Ossuary, a 137 m (449 feet) long gallery-shaped building surrounded by a multitude of white crosses and dominated by a central 46 m (151 feet) high lantern of the dead. The first stone was laid by Philippe Pétain, a man who had experienced firsthand the suffering of Verdun, on August 22, 1920. The Douaumont Ossuary shelters the bones of 130,000 unidentified French and German soldiers who died at Verdun during 1916, and the national military necropolis contains the graves of 16,142 known French soldiers. The remains of 160,000 soldiers, whose bodies were never recovered, rest in the ground that spreads out all around the Douaumont Ossuary. This extensive burial ground remains a protected zone, but bushes and trees have been allowed to grow amongst the trenches and shell craters, sheltering the final resting place of countless men.

Timeline of the Battle of Verdun

1916

February 21: The Battle of Verdun begins with a German preparatory bombardment followed by an infantry assault

Dawn—German artillery bombardment at Verdun begins in preparation for a German infantry assault

4:00 p.m.—The German bombardment ends, and the infantry assault begins. The Bois d'Haumont and the Bois d'Herebois are captured by the Germans, but French Lieutenant Colonel Emile Driant's light infantry regiment just manages to hold on to the Bois des Caures

February 22: The Germans renewed their artillery bombardment at first light. They use a greater contingent of men to attack and overwhelm the defense of the Bois des Caures. The hill is taken, and Emile Driant is shot through the head and dies while withdrawing the remnants of his troops.

February 23: A French counterattack to take the Bois des Caures fails. The village of Brabant is captured, and the defense of Samogneux looks precarious.

February 24: The French second line of defense collapses within a matter of hours. The German advance takes several more key points, pushing the 51st Division off the Bois des Fosses and capturing the village of Ornes on the Meuse.

February 25: Fort Douaumont, the biggest of the mighty forts protecting Verdun, is taken by the German 24th Brandenburg Infantry Regiment, commanded by Lieutenant Eugen Radtke. The French general, Philippe Pétain, an expert in the art of defense, takes command of the Verdun sector and is ordered to hold Verdun whatever the cost.

March 4: The village of Douaumont falls to the Germans, but the German advance slows as the Germans begin to get bogged down in the trenches.

March 6–April 9: Intense fighting continues at Verdun. The German attack on the west bank of the Meuse makes slow but steady progress, capturing Forges, Regnéville, the Bois des Courbeaux (recaptured by the French on the 8 and then lost again on the 9) and Côte de l'Oie. The ridge of Le Mort-Homme still remains in French hands.

April 9: Von Falkenhayn finally allows the Crown Prince to launch a major attack on both sides of the Meuse River. The offensive on the west bank puts German troops on the slopes of Le Mort-Homme (Dead Man's Hill). The offensive on the east bank, however, makes little progress.

April 30: General Philippe Pétain is promoted and takes command of the French Central Army Group. Nivelle becomes commander of the French 2nd Army and takes over the defense of Verdun.

May 4–24: The Germans make repeated attacks on Le Mort-Homme but gain little ground.

May 22: A French counterattack by the 5th Infantry Division to retake Fort Douaumont fails.

May 26: Joffre meets with William Haig at his headquarters and persuades him to move his attack on the Somme from mid-August to the beginning of July.

May 29–June 2: Intense fighting around Côte (Hill) 304, Le Mort-Homme, and Thiaumont continues.

June 3 – 8: Fort Vaux, the second of the great forts of Verdun, is surrounded by the Germans, and after a five-day battle, the French run out of water and are forced to surrender this key site.

June 4: The Russian June Offensive, led by General Brusilov, is launched on the Eastern Front to coincide with the Battle of the Somme. General Brusilov's attack on the Austro-Hungarian Army draws German troops away from Verdun as they are forced to come to the aid of their failing ally.

June 23: The Germans use deadly phosgene gas on the French lines. The German Crown Prince attacks toward Fort Souville, and the Germans come within striking distance of the city of Verdun. The

Germans even fired machine gun bullets into the city streets.

June 23–30: The Germans gain ground after a major German offensive in the Thiaumont–Fleury–Souville sector. But the impending offensive on the Somme begins to divert German attention away from Verdun and toward the Somme.

July 1: The British-led Somme offensive begins farther north and draws German troops away from the continuing Battle of Verdun.

July 11–12: The Germans launch one last desperate attempt to take Verdun, but this final offensive fails to take Souville.

August 28: Falkenhayn resigns and is replaced by the dynamic duo of Paul von Hindenburg and Erich Ludendorff.

September 2: Hindenburg orders that all German offensive operations at Verdun cease.

October 19: The French launch a counteroffensive at Verdun and begin to retake ground that they had lost to the Germans. The French artillery begins a bombardment of the German lines at Verdun.

October 24: The French offensive begins, advancing 3 km (1.8 miles) on the first day, and finally retaking Fort Douaumont.

November 2: French troops retake Fort Vaux.

December 15: French troops push the German forces back almost to their February 1916 position at Bois de Chaume, and the Germans lose nearly all the territory they fought so hard to gain at Verdun.

German and Allied Commanders at the Battle of Verdun

Erich von Falkenhayn – Chief of the German General Staff

Erich von Falkenhayn was the Chief of the German General Staff from September 14, 1914, to August 29, 1916. He chose Verdun as a battleground in an attempt to break the French spirit. Von Falkenhayn was commander of the German army during the Battle of Verdun but was relieved of his command after the Germans failed to take the citadel, despite heavy loss.

Crown Prince Wilhelm – Commander of the German 5th Army at the Battle of Verdun

Crown Prince Wilhelm, the eldest son of Kaiser Wilhelm and the last crown prince of the German Empire, had very little command experience when the First World War broke out, but he was still given command of the 5th

Army in 1914. The Crown Prince was chosen by von Falkenhayn to lead the Germans at the Battle of Verdun at the beginning of 1916. In 1917, Crown Prince Wilhelm, who regarded the war as senseless, tried unsuccessfully to convince the German military leadership to sue for peace. After the war, during his exile in Holland, he was often referred to as the Butcher of Verdun.

Paul von Hindenburg – Commander of the German 8th Army

Paul von Hindenburg was commander of the German 8th Army on the Eastern Front in August 1914. He led his troops to victory over the Russian 2nd Army at the Battle of Tannenberg, and he defeated the Russian 1st Army at the Battle of the Masurian Lakes and successfully pushed the Russians out of East Prussia. For most of the war, he and his second-in-command, General Erich Ludendorff, took control of the army and, in effect, the country. By the end of August, von Falkenhayn was replaced as Chief of the General Staff by Paul von Hindenburg.

Erich Ludendorff – German General

Erich Ludendorff played a key role in ensuring German victory over the Russians at the Battle of Tannenberg; however, he was less successful on the Western Front. Ludendorff ordered the resumption of submarine attacks in the Atlantic, an act that helped convince the Americans to enter the war on the side of the Allies. Ludendorff was Commander Paul von Hindenburg's second-in-command when he took over command of the German forces at the Battle of Verdun.

Philippe Pétain – Marshal of France and Commander-in-Chief of the French forces on the Western Front

Philippe Pétain led the French forces at the Battle of Verdun and was hailed as a national hero for repulsing the German attack. In 1917, he was briefly commander-in-chief of the French Army, and he was able to improve discipline and raise morale at a crucial time in the war for the Allies. Pétain knew how to efficiently organize the defensive line and could pick out key strongpoints that needed to be strengthened. He also realized the value of rotating troops when holding a defensive line in order to keep morale up and avoid exhaustion. Pétain had real compassion for the plight of his men, and it is a tragic irony that he was called upon to subject so many of them to the horror of Verdun.

Joseph Joffre – Marshal of France and Commander-in-Chief of the French forces on the Western Front

Joseph Joffre, nicknamed Papa Joffre, was commander-in-chief of the French forces on the Western Front from the outbreak of the First World War until December 1916. He was hailed by the French as the "Victor of Marne" after France's success at the First Battle of Marne.

Emile Driant – Lieutenant Colonel of the French Army

Emile Driant, a French writer, politician, and army officer, was the first high-ranking

French casualty of the Battle of Verdun. In 1914, he was given command of two infantry battalions, namely the 56th and 59th Chasseurs (French light infantry). In December 1915, he criticized Joffre for removing artillery guns and infantry battalions from Verdun and thus weakening its defenses. He was killed during the Battle of Verdun on February 22, 1916, by a shot through the head while his chasseurs were withdrawing from Bois des Caures. He was initially buried with full military honors by the Germans, but his body was later reinterred where he fell at Bois des Caures. A memorial now stands on the site, and every year on February 21, a ceremony is held honoring Driant and his brave chasseurs. Driant is regarded as a national hero by the French.

Robert Georges Nivelle – General in the French Army

Robert Nivelle served under the command of Philippe Pétain at Verdun until Pétain was promoted to the command of the French Central Army Group in May 1916. Nivelle then took over the command of the French Army at Verdun and led the successful counterattack against the Germans. On December 12, 1916, he was made commander-in-chief of the French armies.

Douglas Haig – British Field Marshal

Douglas Haig was commander-in-chief of the British Expeditionary Forces for most of the First World War. He took over command from John French in 1915. He led the British forces at the Battle of the Somme and the Battle of Passchendaele.

Timeline of Significant Events in the First World War

1914

June 28:   Assassination of Franz Ferdinand

July 28:   The Austro-Hungarian Empire declares war on Serbia

Germany immediately allies itself with the Austro-Hungarian Empire and declares war on Serbia

Russia, in accordance with its alliance with Serbia, begins mobilizing for war on July 29

August 1: Germany declares war on Russia

France is forced to mobilize in accordance with their agreement with Russia

August 3: Germany declares war on France, and German troops pour into neutral Belgium

British Foreign Secretary Sir Edward Grey sends an ultimatum to Germany to withdraw its troops from Belgium

August 4: Germany refuses to withdraw from Belgium

Britain declares war on Germany

August 23: Japan, in accordance with an alliance signed with Britain in 1902, declares war on Germany

August 4–September 6: Battle of the Frontiers

August 26 -30: Battle of Tannenberg

September 6-10: First Battle of Marne

October 19: Start of the First Battle of Ypres

October 29: The Ottoman Empire (modern-day Turkey) enters the war on the side of the Central Powers and assists Germany in a naval bombardment of Russia

November 2: Russia declares war on the Ottoman Empire

November 5: Britain and France declare war on the Ottoman Empire

November 22: End of the First Battle of Ypres

December 24–25: Christmas Truce on the Western Front

1915

February 19: Start of the naval bombardment of the Dardanelles

March 18: End of the naval bombardment of the Dardanelles

April 22: Start of the Second Battle of Ypres

April 25: Start of Gallipoli Campaign

May 7: German U-Boat sinks the Lusitania

May 23: Italy joins the war on the side of the Allies

May 25: End of the Second Battle of Ypres

September 25: Start of the Battle of Loos

October 8: End of the Battle of Loos

1916

January 9: End of Gallipoli Campaign

February 21: Start of the Battle of Verdun

May 31–June 1: Battle of Jutland

June 4: The Russian June Offensive, including the Brusilov Offensive, is launched on the Eastern Front to coincide with the Battle of the Somme

July 1: Start of the Battle of the Somme

September 20: End of the Russian Offensive

November 18: End of the Battle of the Somme

December 18: End of the Battle of Verdun

1917

March 15: Tsar Nicholas is forced to abdicate from the Russian throne, ending 304 years of Romanov rule

 Tsar Nicholas is replaced by a provisional government

April 6: The United States of America joins the war

July 1-19: Russian July Offensive (Kerensky Offensive) on the Eastern Front

November 6-7: Revolution breaks out in Russia, and the provisional government is overthrown by the Bolsheviks

1918

March 3: Russia signs the Treaty of Brest-Litovsk with the Central Powers, and war ends in Russia

July 17: Tsar Nicholas and his family are murdered at Yekaterinburg

August 8: Start of the Hundred Day Offensive

November 11: The First World War officially ends on the eleventh hour of the eleventh day of the eleventh month